HENRY
HUDSON

HENRY HUDSON

Joan Joseph

A Visual Biography
Illustrated with authentic prints, documents, and maps

Franklin Watts, Inc. / New York / 1974

For Len

Historical consultant,
Professor Richard Whittemore
Teachers College, Columbia University

Original maps and drawings by William K. Plummer

Library of Congress Cataloging in Publication Data

Joseph, Joan.
  Henry Hudson.

  (A Visual biography)
  SUMMARY: A biography of the explorer who
claimed the Hudson Valley for the Dutch and the
Hudson bay area for the English.
  1. Hudson, Henry, d. 1611—Juvenile literature.
[1. Hudson, Henry, d. 1611. 2. Explorers] I. Title.
E129.H8J67   974.7'3'010924 [B] [92] 73-14704
ISBN 0-531-01276-X

        3   4   5   6   7   8   9   10

A Note on the Illustrations

This book is illustrated with pictures that were drawn about the time that Henry Hudson lived. They show us how England looked at that time, and how the first Europeans to see the New World pictured it and the people they found living there. There are a number of maps from this period reproduced in this book. They reveal the changes that were taking place in people's knowledge of the New World.

The maps drawn by William K. Plummer for this book are marked with the initials WKP.

Illustration credits

The British Museum: pp. ii, 8A & B,
11, 19A, 20, 31, 37, 40, 45, 46, 48
Radio Times Hulton Picture Library:
pp. vi, 3A, 12, 15, 19B, 23A, & B, 28
The London Museum: pp. 3B, 6

*The city of London
in the 1600s.*

AN ENGLISH SEAMAN

A cloud of mystery surrounds Henry Hudson. In the first place, no one knows what this famous explorer looked like. He may have been tall and thin, or perhaps he was short and extremely robust; he may have been bald or he may have had thick, wavy hair. We can imagine him with dark, pensive eyes or we can visualize him with sharp, blue-green eyes. So remember, when you look at a portrait of Captain Henry Hudson, it has been painted from the imagination of the artist; it is not a likeness of that great sea captain who helped shape England's far-flung empire.

Only four years, from January 1607 to June 23, 1611, of the exciting story of Henry Hudson are actually recorded in history. Before then, we can only try to piece together the details of his life. We know that he lived in London near the gloomy fortress called the Tower of London. In this frightening prison nobles and even queens were executed.

Hudson married a woman named Katherine — her maiden name has never been discovered — and they had three sons: Oliver, John, and Richard. After the first son, Oliver, was married, his first child, Alice, was born in 1608. At the christening of Alice, we know that her uncle Richard (Henry's son) was about three years old; and John, who accompanied his father on his voyages, is believed at the time of the christening to have been entering his teens. This scanty information that is available about the family suggests that Henry Hudson was born sometime around 1575.

Although personal facts of Hudson's early life are not known, it is not difficult to re-create a picture of the London of his youth. Henry Hudson is believed to have been the grandson of an alderman — a member of the council of the city of London — also named Henry Hudson. Since we know that he was born into an educated family, and that he could read and write, it seems reasonable to assume that he was one of the fortunate youngsters of those days who went to school. In sixteenth-century England, only boys attended school. The few girls who received an education studied with private tutors. The boys' classes were held in summer and winter and the school day lasted from seven in the morning until five in the afternoon; their lunch period, however, was usually two hours long. Reading, writing, and arithmetic were of primary importance, but a fluent knowledge of Latin was considered a necessary part of a gentleman's education. Greek was also taught to the boys as was history and geography. The headmaster was expected to be very stern, and strict discipline was considered the most important lesson in a boy's development.

Hudson was born during the reign of Queen Elizabeth I. Elizabethan England, also Shakespeare's England, was the home of the "Elizabethan Sea Dogs": men like the famous navigator Sir Francis Drake, the first Englishman to sail around the world; and Sir Richard Hawkins, who accompanied Drake on the first half of his memorable voyage.

It was also during this period that the well-known English geographer, Richard Hakluyt, introduced the use of globes into the English schools. There is no question that Hakluyt, who

*Above, the Tower of London
with shipping on the Thames.
Below, spectators watching
a cock fight.*

was later in close contact with Hudson, influenced him greatly, as did the general interest of sixteenth-century scholars in world geography. For Hudson was only one of many who dreamed of finding a short route to the rich ports of the Orient.

Hudson grew up in a country that was undergoing a great cultural revolution. Theater had become a popular pastime; this was the only period in England's history when she ranked as the leader of music in Europe. Spectator sports were also extremely popular. There were tennis matches and jousting tournaments. Bull- and bear-baiting arenas were built and the people of London were enthusiastic fans of these gruesome matches where powerful dogs, known as mastiffs attacked chained bears and bulls, clawing and biting the poor animals until they collapsed. These matches were so popular that they were often held, by order of the queen, to entertain foreign dignitaries. Cock fights were another popular entertainment.

Just as the people enjoyed watching violence in the arena, so did they enjoy watching it on the stage. Although the plays of the period, including Shakespeare's, were filled with lessons concerning moral conduct, violent action was very much a part of sixteenth-century theater; and the people's taste for blood and gore was further satisfied when they were allowed to watch the execution of a criminal.

While Hudson was growing up, the city of London was hardly an ideal place to live. The streets were strewn with garbage, which was guarded by well-fed rats and swarms of flies. There were no garbage collectors in those days; only the rains cleaned away the rotting food that lay in the middle of the dark, narrow, cobblestone streets. The people of London, as elsewhere, did not realize that by throwing food out of their windows and allowing it to rot in the streets, they were endangering their lives. They had no idea that their way of living helped keep alive the treacherous little fleas that, over a period of a hundred years, carried Bubonic Plague from one port of Europe to another.

In the fall of 1592, the plague struck London. The epidemic threatened the life of every Londoner and in fact, 10 percent of the population died. It was a horrible disease that caused raging fevers and excruciating pain. In Europe it was called the "black death," because the bodies of the unfortunate victims turned black. There was no cure for the black death, and the people, realizing that the diseased victims were contagious, cast their rotting black bodies out into the streets to die. It must have been a ghastly sight to watch the dead being collected and carried away in carts to special burying places. Londoners knew that those who were infected helped spread the plague; they had no idea that the monstrous rats, who made their home along the wharves, were the real villains. The rats seemed to inspect each new vessel that arrived in London, and it was in these ships that the fleas that carried the plague made their home. The fleas attached themselves to the rats, and when the black rodents waddled back to town, they spread the disease wherever they went. "The cause of plagues is sin," the preachers of London declared, "and the cause of sin is plays." When the plague struck, all public meeting places were forced to close. Crowds were supposedly prohibited for reasons of health, but the people were allowed to gather at church. Even those who were not religious believed that the sin of the people had aroused God's anger and that God alone could drive away the black death.

As a boy, Hudson is believed to have lived near the docks of London. Though the streets may have been no place to play, living along the banks of the Thames was ideal for a boy interested in the sea; he could talk to the sailors and listen to their wonderful tales of exotic ports. And for a youngster who dreamt of sailing, it must have been thrilling to be able to watch the impressive

ee Last Great Years of Past
every Parish in the said Years
1665. bein... rue Account how many Persons died Weekly in every of those Years, also how
Figures of ... Greatness of the CALAMITY, and the Violence of the DISTEMPER in the Last Year,

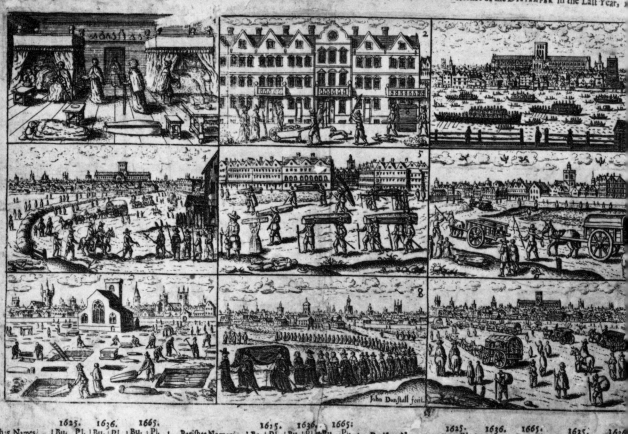

John Dunstall fecit.

three-masted ships as the wind filled their square-rigged sails and carried them out to sea.

Hudson's love of the sea is quite understandable, for he was born into a family of seamen. His grandfather, Alderman Hudson, helped the explorer Sebastian Cabot found the Muscovy Company. This company, also called the Russia Company, was established in the hope of promoting the discovery of a northeasterly water route to the Indies. We know that a Christopher Hudson was an agent of the company in Russia, and that under the company, a Captain Thomas Hudson commanded an expedition to Persia. There are written records proving that this Captain Hudson advised John Davys in his search for a passage to China. It was this voyage that led to the discovery of Davys (also Davis) Strait and it was here, Davys wrote in 1587, that "we saw the sea falling down into a gulf with a mighty overfall and moving with diverse motions like whirlpools." Davys called these rushing waters the Furious Overfall, and his description of the swift currents caught Hudson's curiosity. Hudson was a scientist as well as an explorer, and once he heard of the Furious Overfall he was determined to find out what caused the frantic motion of the water. The more he studied, the more he became convinced that beyond the spinning whirlpools lay an inland waterway to the Pacific.

Some historians claim that Hudson had sailed with Davys and had seen the Furious Overfall. But there is no proof to back this claim; even the details of the voyage described in "Henry Hudson's Journal for 1587" are questionable. Many scholars believe it is a forgery, and even in the seventeenth century, a number of writers accused Hudson's eldest son, Oliver, of having written the journal after his father's death.

A record in pictures of the plague in London, giving the numbers killed by the disease in the 1600s.

C ROCLAND

GROENLAND

NORTH

ISELAND

IAFLAN

TARRY ILANDES

NORWAY

ME

C OVNTS OF SVSSEX MYNE
WINTERS FORNACE
COVNTS OF WARWICKE YLAD
OWENS MOVND
HADON NESTES
BEARS SOVND
LOCKES LAND
COLE
ERLE OF SVSSEXYLE
HALLESTLAND

C WALSINGHAM

SCHETLAND

SWETH

WEST INGLAND
OLIM WEST FRISELAND

GNI

THE WAY TRENDING TO CATHAIA

FROBISSHERS STREIGHTS

CHARINE CROSSE

EST

THE

QVEN ELI: FOR LAND

T   A C: BEST
T MOVNT OXFORD HATTONS HEADLAND

IRELAND

SCOTLAND

INGLAND

FRA

WEST

MISTAKEN STRAIGHTES

FRANC

SYPPOSED FRILAND OF AMERICA

AMERICA

SOVTH

Whether or not Hudson wrote the journal is unimportant; nor does it matter where Hudson had sailed in his youth. The most important fact is that by 1607, when the name of Henry Hudson first appears in the history of England, he had already established himself as an outstanding sea captain. We know this, because in January of that year he is described in the minutes of a meeting of the Muscovy Company as "an experienced seapilot . . . who has in his possession secret information that will enable him to find the north-east passage."

And we also know that by 1607 Hudson had already determined that he would be remembered in the pages of history as a great explorer. For shortly after he received his appointment from the company, he wrote to the famous geographer Richard Hakluyt: "I would take leave of England in a few months to test the theory that a route to Cathay can be found across the half-frozen seas that cover the roof of the world. I shall come to you at Bristol, and with your permission shall study your charts of that region. . . . If the route be not found to the north, I know another. Would there were at [my] disposal all that others have gleaned about my Furious Overfall in the western sea. There, I know, lies the sure sea path to the Indies, and he who finds it will be remembered for all time, even as Drake will not be forgot. I pray with all my heart. Be it by northern path or western, I would that my name be carved on the tablets of the sea."

Above, the Ark Royal, *flagship of Queen Elizabeth's navy in the late 1500s. Below, a map of the unknown area of the north, drawn in 1578. This map was one of the principal sources of Hudson's belief that there was a northwest passage.*

ACROSS THE TOP OF THE WORLD

The directors of the Muscovy Company believed that Hudson knew of a secret route whereby a ship could sail across the North Pole to China and Japan. In those days, a round-trip voyage to the Orient could take as long as three years. If Hudson were right, the company knew that they could send ships to the Orient and back in one season. This, of course, meant that their costs would be lower and their earnings would increase tremendously.

Had the directors been well informed, however, they would have realized that Hudson's plan was neither original nor secret. As early as 1527, Robert Thorne had come up with the idea that a northern waterway existed across the Pole to Cathay, as China was called in the sixteenth century. He had presented his scheme to King Henry VIII, but the reigning monarch had had no faith in the plan. In 1599, Thorne's letter was published. This was the secret information that Hudson had in his possession. But until this time, no one had ever tested Thorne's theory that "there is no land uninhabitable and no sea unnavigable."

While Hudson was in Bristol, we know that Hakluyt showed him a letter written by the outstanding Dutch geographer, Peter Plancius, in which he stated with certainty that: "Near the Pole the sun shines for five months continually; and though its rays

"First problems of sailing by Mercator's chart." This manuscript was studied by Hudson as he was planning his voyages.

Of Saileng by Mercators Chart.

Lett there begiven Lizard N Latt: 50° 00ʹ & and Barbadoes N latt 13° 16ʹ N long: 52° 58ʹ &
there be required the course and distance from Lizard to Barbadoes by Mercators Chart.

Upon the Meridian line extend the Compass from the Lat: of Lizard to the Latitude of Barbadoes
& that same extent to the Equinochall & you shall find it to be 44° 37ʹ for the difference
Latitude enlarged or which is all one the difference of latitude in meridionall parts which
... in Leagues and lay from A to B in the figure ~~...~~ & through
point B draw BC parallel to A E & thereon lay the difference of longitude from B to C &
... A E.

Next lay the difference of latitude in leagues from A to F and draw F G parallel to
... A E.

Then A represents Lizard, C Barbadoes by Mercators Chart AB the difference of Latitude
enlarged or in meridionall parts BC the difference of long: in meridionall parts A F the true
... of latitude in leagues F G the meridian distance or difference of longitude in leagues
the point G is the place of Barbadoes by the globe.

Then to find the Course saye

As the difference of Latitude in meridionall parts — A B — 0892.
Is to the difference of longitude in meridionall parts   B C — 1059.
Soe is Radius — — — — — — — — —   — .....
To the tangent of the Course 49 — — — — — — — 19. 55. S 38ʹ 4° 55ʹ 38ʹ
E

Then for the meridian distance

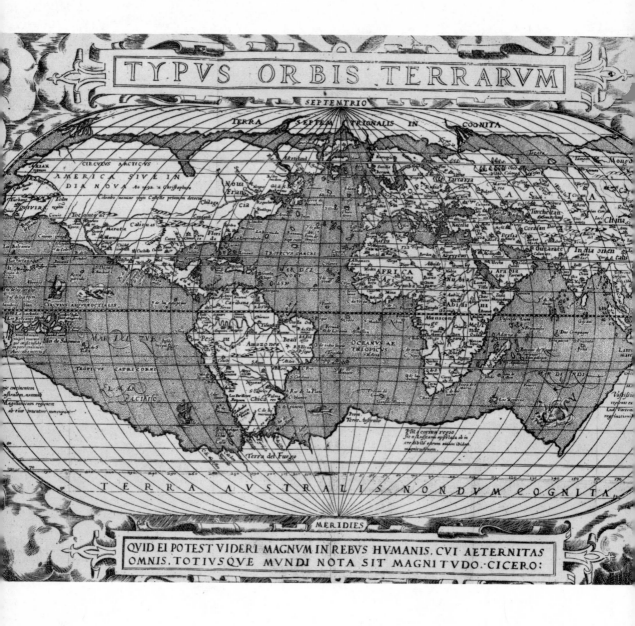

*A map of the world contained in
some copies of the first edition of
Hakluyt's* Principles of Navigation, *1589.*

are weak . . . they have sufficient strength to warm the ground (the Pole itself being an island surrounded by sea)." Plancius's theory was further supported by another clergyman-geographer, Reverend Samuel Purchas, who claimed that the Pole was only a point and "If either by North-east or North-west or North a passage be open," — that is if the point was not blocked by land — a sea voyage across the top of the world "with much ease and in little time and expense might be effected."

Before leaving Bristol, Hudson wrote to the directors of the Muscovy Company stating that he had completed his studies, mapped out his journey, and was ready to "depart across the 'Point' to the Sea of Chin [the China Sea]" — the gateway to the fabulous Cipangu [Japan], where the streets were paved with precious stones and the emperor lived in a palace covered with shining sheets of pure gold.

Was it the wealth of Cipangu that influenced Hudson when he agreed to accept the company's meager offer of £135 5s. as the fee for his voyage? This sum, today equivalent to about $325, had a value at that time of approximately $3,500. This was hardly enough money to compensate for the tremendous risks the voyage entailed. Or, was money unimportant to Hudson? Was he only interested in his dream — in those words he had confided to Hakluyt when he wrote: "I would that my name be carved on the tablets of the sea"?

THE FIRST TWO VOYAGES

On April 19, 1607, Henry Hudson, his middle son, John, and his ten-member crew attended a special farewell service in the small sanctuary of St. Ethelburgh Church in London. From there they proceeded to the docks and boarded the *Hopewell*, the 80-ton ship that the company had outfitted for Hudson's first voyage.

We do not have a description of the *Hopewell*, but like the other ships of this period, it was undoubtedly a flat-bottomed boat with a high bow and stern. Square rigging and square sails were used then, and the construction of the hulls made a ship rock in even a slightly turbulent sea. It could hardly have been an ideal vessel for sailing the rough waters of the Arctic.

Due to heavy fog, the men were forced to delay their trip thirteen days; at last, on May 1, the skies cleared and Hudson gave the order to weigh anchor and cast off. His first great voyage was underway.

Hudson's careful records of his trips were of great value to future seamen. He was one of the first mariners to establish the tradition of keeping a daily log of a ship's travels. This was an important step in the advancement of navigation, for it meant that the records of a voyage would be available for other navigators to study. Hudson was the first Englishman to record the fact that the needle of the compass is affected by the magnetic pole, an important scientific observation. "This day I found the needle to incline 79° under the Horizon," he wrote on May 30.

From his log, we know that balmy weather and favorable

*St. Ethelburgh Church in the
Bishopsgate section of London.*

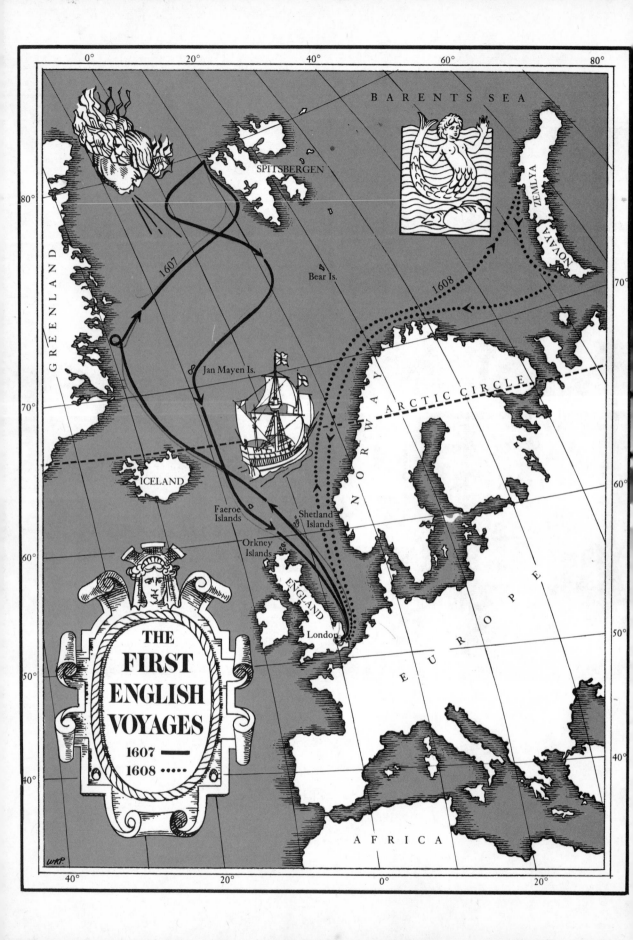

BARENTS SEA

SPITSBERGEN

ZEMLYA

NOVAYA

GREENLAND

1607

Bear Is.

1608

70°

80°

ARCTIC CIRCLE

Jan Mayen Is.

NORWAY

EUROPE

ICELAND

Faeroe
Islands

Shetland
Islands

Orkney
Islands

ENGLAND

London

THE
FIRST
ENGLISH
VOYAGES

1607 ——
1608 ······

EUROPE

60°

50°

40°

AFRICA

0°   20°   40°   60°   80°

40°   20°   0°   20°

wkp

winds accompanied the *Hopewell* throughout the month of May. It sailed along a steady course pushing northward past the Shetland and Faroe Islands, skirting the shores of Iceland and heading toward the bleak coast of Greenland. Then, suddenly, during the second week of June, the ship passed out of the calm waters. Icebergs loomed ahead, endangering the little vessel which was being tossed about by gale winds. Day after day, Hudson recorded the terrible conditions. From the eleventh until the twentieth of June his words barely changed: "a fresh gale all night . . . a stiff gale . . . all the night; a great fog with much wind. . . ." on the nineteenth, "the fog increased very thick, with much wind. . . ." Finally, on the twentieth of June, "at two in the afternoon, it cleared up and we saw the sun."

The *Hopewell* was off the coast of Greenland. Hudson, believing that he had discovered a new land named it "Hold-with-Hope." But he could hardly have been filled with hope, for he had believed Greenland was just off the coast of Norway and that beyond it there was an open sea which would lead to the Orient. He realized that this voyage had been unsuccessful and in his log, he seemed to try to justify his trip to the directors of the company. "We did cling to this coast of Greenland . . ." he wrote, "realizing that it was unknown to the seamen of all European nations. We did find land in many places where my charts showed nothing but sea. Therefore our time was not greatly wasted."

Having charted the 1,500 mile coast of Greenland, Hudson, still hoping to find a passage, steered the *Hopewell* northeasterly, reaching Spitsbergen (a group of islands off the coast of Norway) at the end of June. Hudson spent the next two weeks cruising between the islands. On the morning of July 14, 1607, when he sailed into the placid harbor he named "Whales Bay," without realizing it he was assuring his place in history. William Barents, a Dutch explorer, had discovered Spitsbergen in 1596, but it was

Hudson who brought back a description of these waters, teeming with hundreds of mammoth whales. "There are more whales in the bay than ever any man could number," he wrote.

Late that night, the crew hoisted the anchor and sailed northward. Within two days they found themselves almost completely surrounded by ice. They had reached the Great Ice Barrier and were forced to turn south. Once freed from the ice, the *Hopewell* sailed on a direct course back to England. Hudson was certain that his voyage had been a complete failure. In the closing pages of the ship's log he wrote: "I have searched long and diligently for a Passage to China by the North Pole. Now I can assure others that . . . there is no such Passage. Yet I think one day Spitsbergen, which I have now examined, may be profitable to those who have the courage to develop it."

The *Hopewell* docked in London on September 15, and almost overnight, the shares of the Muscovy Company tripled in value. Hudson's description of Whales Bay had brought about a booming new industry in England. Until this time, the whaling industry had been solely in the hands of the Basques — the Spanish and French living on the shores of the Bay of Biscay. Now England, and before the end of the year most of Europe, planned to exploit the Arctic whale.

Both the blubber and bones of the whale were of great commercial value. Oil extracted from the blubber was used in making soap, was burned in lamps, and was excellent to grease carriage wheels and other mechanical moving parts. Whale bones were particularly in demand for the rigid corsets that were then fashionable.

When the first whaling ship was ready to sail, the company asked Hudson to lead the expedition. Hudson refused. He agreed to act as an adviser but explained that he was an explorer, not a whale hunter. At the same time, however, he requested permission from the directors to lead a second expedition in search of a northerly passage to the East. The directors considered Hudson's

Left, a woman of Greenland, with
her baby. A painting by John White,
1577. Below, a Dutch woodcut
showing early whaling techniques

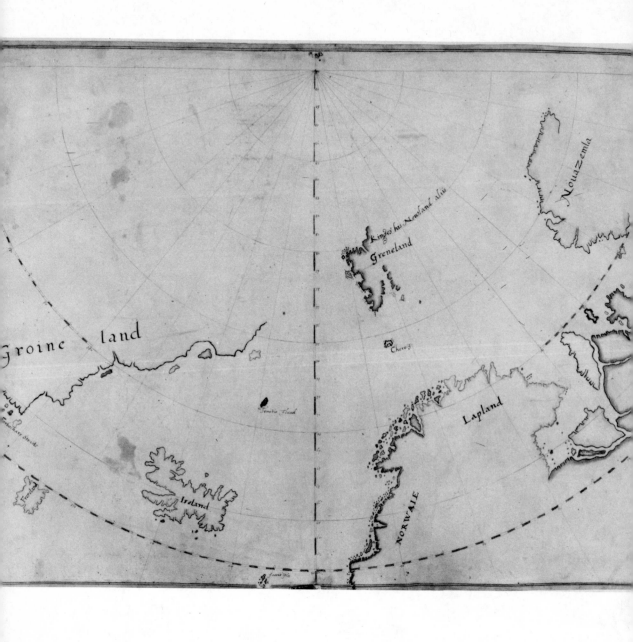

*A map of Greenland, as it was
known before Hudson's explorations.*

first voyage a total failure, but because the company had become so prosperous, they agreed to finance a second venture.

Hudson's new contract was much the same as his first one. He was to sail in the *Hopewell* and, as before, the pay was minimal. This time, however, he was allowed to hire four additional crew members.

Once again, John accompanied his father, but Hudson only rehired two seamen. We are not certain whether he wanted to make such a complete change, or if his original crew were unavailable. There is no doubt that many of that crew turned from exploring to whale hunting.

The sailors that accompanied Hudson on his second trip were a rough group. Hudson, now knowing the dangers of the Arctic waters, wanted the strongest men he could enlist. As his firstmate he chose Robert Juet because "Juet," he wrote to Hakluyt, "is filled with mean tempers." Juet was an extremely experienced mariner, but his own journal reveals that from the very beginning, he disliked Hudson. He was jealous of the captain and hated taking orders from a man twelve to fifteen years younger than he. Juet was fifty years old at the time of the second voyage.

The preparations for this voyage were made more carefully than were those for the first. Hudson had the hull of the *Hopewell* reinforced with extra planks to protect it from the treacherous ice. He ordered thicker masts and insisted upon taking a sturdier and larger row boat for shore excursions. He stored larger quantities of dried beans and pork and carried muskets for every man as well as a small cannon for his own use. By April 22, 1608, the *Hopewell* was ready to sail.

This time Hudson, having given up the idea of sailing across the Pole, was searching for a northeast passage to the Orient. Misled by the charts and maps of the day, he plotted his course around the northern Cape of Norway, hoping to discover a passage through the Russian island of Novaya Zemlya. On the eastern side of the island lay the Kara Sea, and according to rumor — which Hudson believed to be true — once he rounded the legendary Cape of Tabin, he would come upon warm waters perfumed by "incense-bearing trees."

By the end of May, the *Hopewell* was off the west coast of Norway. The winds were favorable, but the progress of the ship was slowed down by thick fog. Once she was around the North Cape, however, the fog lifted and by the first week of June the little vessel entered the Barents Sea. Hudson, carrying the newest available equipment, measured the depth of the sea. Soundings — measurements of the depth made with a weighted line — on the first day indicated that the sea's floor was 150 fathoms below water level; the following day, they could not find the bottom at 180 fathoms. Hudson noted in his journal that he was certain that he had found a deep-water channel to the Orient. The next morning, he realized what really lay ahead. On his first voyage he had observed that "the sea was blue in color when there was ice and green where it was open." On June 9, the sea was blackish-blue. Within twenty-four hours, the first chunks of floating ice were sighted.

Although other mariners may have noticed the change in the color of the water when there was ice in an area, Hudson was the first to record his observations, which proved to be scientifically correct.

The *Hopewell* had reached the Great Ice Barrier again. It was impossible for Hudson to maintain a northerly course. Much to his dismay, he was forced to steer his ship southeasterly.

Above, a navigation instrument made for Francis Drake in 1596. Below, a voyage to Spitzbergen in the late 1600s.

22

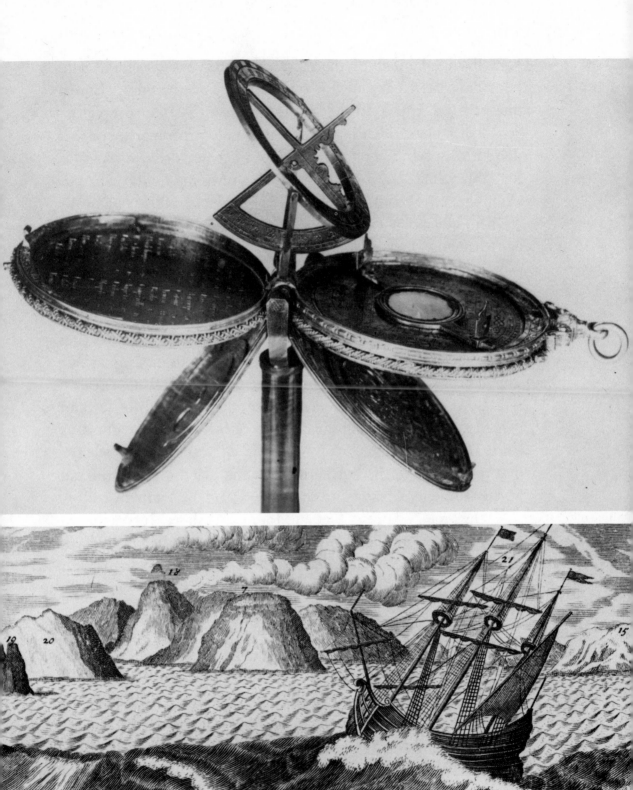

Then came one of the most exciting moments of the trip. Four days later, on June 15, two members of the crew claimed they saw a mermaid. In the seventeenth century most people believed that mermaids existed, and it is not surprising, therefore, that Hudson felt it important to write a detailed description in his log: "She came close to the ship, looking earnestly on the men. . . . From the navel upward her back and breasts were like a woman's . . . her body as big as one of us; her skin very white, and her long hair, hanging down behind, of color black; in her going down they saw her tail, which was like the tail of a porpoise and speckled like a mackerel."

Then, three days later, the *Hopewell* was again face to face with the Great Ice Barrier. "We heard bears make their roaring on the ice," Hudson wrote, "they came close to gaze upon our ship; and we also saw upon the ice . . . a great number of seals."

By mid-June Hudson gave up fighting the fields of ice and turned eastward, reaching the coast of Novaya Zemlya eight days later. He realized immediately that the ice was far too thick for him to sail around the northern tip of the island, but he still had hopes of finding a passage to the Kara Sea at the southern end.

On June 27 he sent Juet and four men ashore. Juet returned with news that on the island the sun was warm, the grass green, and there were even white and pink flowers blooming. He brought back a number of deer antlers and spoke of trackings in the soggy ground that looked like the footmarks of deer and fox.

Hudson was more certain than ever that the land of the midnight sun had a temperate climate and therefore, must contain an ice-free waterway leading to the East. He continued his fruitless search for another week. But on the evening of July 5, he seemed to give up: "Tomorrow morning," he wrote, "we will set sail and stand to the westward, being out of hope to find a passage to the north-east." When the crew realized that Hudson was steering due west, there was near mutiny aboard under Juet's leadership. But before Juet could work out a plan, Hudson agreed to return home.

On August 26, 1608 the *Hopewell* reached England. There was no doubt in anyone's mind that the voyage had been a total failure. Hudson was dismissed from the service of the company; he was depressed by his failure, and no one could convince him that his trip had been worthwhile.

THE *HALF MOON* ON THE HUDSON

The directors of the Muscovy Company had lost all interest in Hudson, and English merchants, in general, were unwilling to risk their funds to back an explorer they regarded as a total failure. The Reverend Samuel Purchas met Hudson several times during the following months. "He had sunk into the lowest depths of the Humor of Melancholy, from which no man could rouse him," he later wrote. "It mattered not that his perseverance and industry had made England the richer by his maps of the North. I told him he had created Fame that would endure for all time, but he would not listen to me."

Then, in the last week of October 1608, the Dutch Consul in London, Emanuel van Meteran, acting as the representative of the Dutch East India Company, invited Hudson to Holland. The directors of the company appreciated that Hudson was an outstanding navigator as well as a man of great courage. It was Hudson's good fortune that the directors were searching for a route to the East that would allow their ships to sail with complete freedom from Spanish and Portuguese interference. They hoped that Hudson would be the one to discover a short northern route to the Orient.

The trip from London to Holland on a cross-Channel packet boat was a rough one. Hudson, though a hardy mariner, had to fight against seasickness. "The odours below deck were so offensive to my nostrils," he wrote to his wife, Katherine, "that I begged the captain for the privilege of standing on his quarterdeck so I would not become ill."

Upon his arrival in Holland, Hudson delayed meeting with the company directors so that he could visit the famous geographer, Reverend Peter Plancius. Plancius, a Belgian emigrant, had opened a school of navigation in Amsterdam and his influence was responsible for the early voyages of the Dutch in the Atlantic waters. The directors of the Dutch East India Company were not impressed with Hudson's plan and decided that it would be a poor investment.

Plancius did not give Hudson time to brood. Instead, he immediately approached the French government and explained that Hudson believed in the existence of a northern passage to the East. When the Dutch directors heard that the French were considering financing Hudson's next voyage, they lost no time in drawing up a contract; it was signed on January 8, 1609.

This time Hudson received even less money than before. The Dutch company paid him the equivalent of sixty-five English pounds, and in the event that he did not return, they agreed to give an additional sixteen pounds to his wife.

For this third, and what proved to be his most important voyage, Hudson was to sail the *Half Moon* (or Halve Maen in Dutch), a ship that was twenty tons lighter than the *Hopewell*. The sixty-ton *Half Moon* was in such poor condition that Hudson wrote to the directors, stating: "I fear she will prove difficult to handle in foul weather." "The *Half Moon* is the only ship at the disposal of the Dutch East India Company," the company director replied, "if you do not want the *Half Moon*, the Company will be obliged to find another Captain to carry out this assignment."

Hudson had no choice; even an old ship was better than no ship at all. He was determined to find a northern passage to Cathay. Although he may have been disgruntled, he continued to prepare for the trip.

According to his contract Hudson could hire eighteen seamen. Unfortunately, his choice of crew could hardly have been worse. For some unknown reason he rehired Robert Juet as his

An imaginative painting
of Hudson's Half Moon.

first mate. No one has been able to understand why Hudson wanted to sail a second time with a man who had tried to lead a mutiny against him. There is no record listing the crew, but we do know that John Coleman, Hudson's mate on his first voyage, was aboard; and Hudson's son, John, was listed as a passenger. The other crew members were a mixture of Dutch and English seamen. Hudson, who did not speak Dutch, hired Jodocus Hondius as his interpreter. Hondius was both a distinguished sculptor and an outstanding map maker. And although his maps most certainly aided Hudson in charting his course, he was of little assistance in helping his captain choose his crew. Hondius's only experience at sea was as a passenger and, therefore, he had no way of determining whether or not the men he interviewed would be suitable sailors.

Only a few pages of the journal of Hudson's third voyage have survived the centuries. We know that the *Half Moon* left Amsterdam on April 6, 1609; and from the diaries of Juet and Coleman, we know that storms beset the ship from the outset and that the *Half Moon* took a month to reach the coast of Norway.

The fact that the Dutch and English sailors could not understand each other was a constant source of trouble, and once the little craft began to be tossed about in the stormy seas, the language barrier became a serious problem. Each group banned together against the other and the English seamen not only resented the Dutch, but were afraid they were planning to mutiny.

Hudson had chosen experienced Dutch sailors, but their previous voyages had been to the warm waters of the East Indies. They had never been exposed to the howling gales and rough waters of the North Sea. They became seasick almost at once, collapsing in their hammocks and refusing to partake in any outdoor chores. By the time the *Half Moon* reached the North Cape of Norway, the situation had become unbearable. The fact that there was near mutiny aboard, however, was to Hudson's advantage. He had sworn to the directors that he would search for a northeast passage to the Orient; his dream was to sail westward. He had studied the foremost maps and charts of the period, such as Mercator's map and Michael Lok's charts. These clearly showed the existence of a northwestern passage to the East; furthermore, Captain John Smith, founder of England's empire in North America, had written to Hudson that north of Jamestown, Virginia, was a sea leading to the western ocean. From the outset of this voyage Hudson had wanted to explore this theory; now he had his chance. The crew all agreed that he should disobey orders and sail west.

And so, in the last week of May 1609, Hudson charted a new course, heading westward past the coast of Greenland toward the shores of northern Maine. The weather was good and the winds were favorable and by June 19 they reached the banks of Newfoundland. It must be remembered that this Newfoundland was not the large island in the mouth of the St. Lawrence River, but was the Continental Shelf off the coast of northern Maine and eastern Canada; the great banks of New-found-waters teeming with codfish and herrings.

In the first five hours after their arrival the crew caught 118 large cod. The following day, however, they encountered a fleet of French fishermen. The French had long since claimed the banks as their domain and Hudson, not wishing to start trouble, directed his ship southward. Heavy fog delayed their progress, but at last, on July 17, the *Half Moon* anchored in Penobscot Bay, Maine.

Hudson's arrival in the New World did not go unnoticed: "six Indians paddling in two birch bark canoes came out to us," Juet wrote in his diary, "seeming glad of our coming. . . .They ate and drank with us . . . and one of them spoke some words of

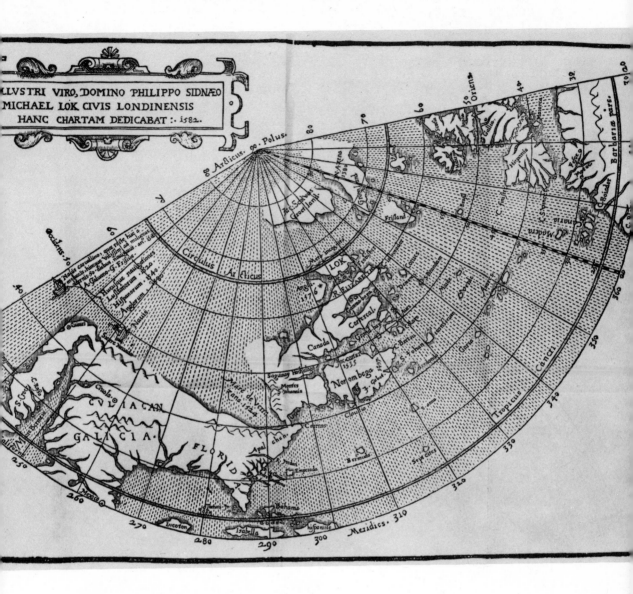

A map of the New World
by Michael Lok, 1582.

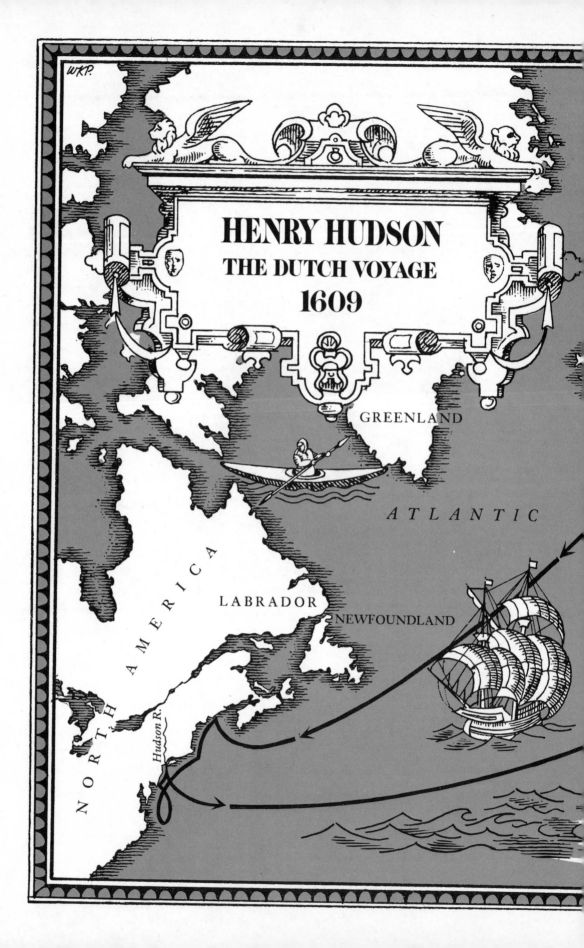

HENRY HUDSON
THE DUTCH VOYAGE
1609

GREENLAND

ATLANTIC

LABRADOR

NEWFOUNDLAND

NORTH AMERICA

Hudson R.

WKP.

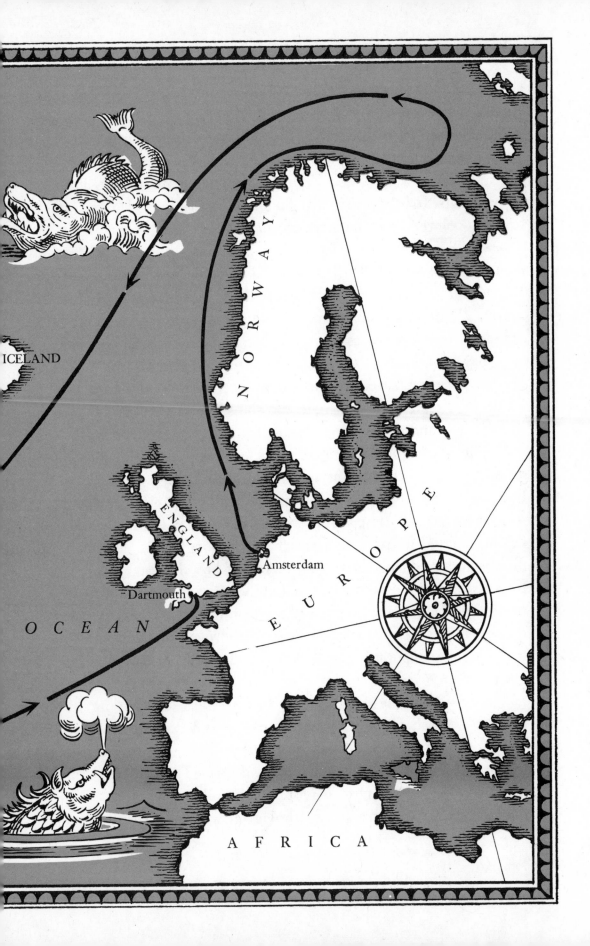

French." But even if some conversation was exchanged, their discussions were probably carried on in sign language and pantomime. Hudson gave the Indians blankets, beads, and mirrors as a sign of friendship. The following day, the Indians returned with fox and beaver skins. They could hardly have realized the value of their furs, for they virtually gave them away in exchange for brightly colored nightshirts which they called "red gowns."

On July 18, 1609, Hudson, accompanied by a few of his men, went ashore for the first time. "The wilderness of the New World forms a vast natural cathedral," Hudson wrote in his journal. "No work of man is equal. Nowhere is there such natural grandeur. In many places the forest comes down to meet the sea, ... I did not know whether to weep or cry aloud with joy. ..." Hudson was enchanted by the woods of Maine. Wanting to be alone, he dispatched his men to the ship, "myself remaining on shore...till sundown,...then Juet sent my boat to fetch me...."

The *Half Moon* remained at anchor until July 24, when a group of crew members attacked a nearby Indian camp. The Indians, unaccustomed to firearms, fled into the forest and the seamen looted the camp. Hudson was aware of what happened, yet he omitted it from his journal and although Juet described the skirmish in detail, there is no record of how Hudson reacted. If he disapproved of his men's conduct, he certainly made no effort to control them; he neither punished them nor made them return the stolen furs. It almost seems as if he approved of their action, for the following morning at 5 A.M., the *Half Moon* quietly sailed on.

The weeks ahead proved to be the most outstanding of Hudson's career. He was by no means the first explorer in these waters, and he knew it. When he reached Cape Cod, he did not hesitate to record in his log that he had arrived at the headland discovered by the English explorer, Captain Batholomew Gosnold, in 1602. Hudson's voyage, however, was of far greater importance to the field of exploration than Gosnold's, for Hudson was the first mariner to chart the New England coastline in detail.

The *Half Moon* sailed as far south as the coast of Virginia. Based on Lok's chart, however, Hudson seemed certain that the inland water route, connecting the Atlantic to the Pacific, could not be so far south. When he turned his ship northward, he could hardly have known that two weeks later, on September 2, 1609, the dream of his life would be fulfilled. On that morning, as he sailed past the beaches of Sandy Hook to the southern tip of the island that became known as Manhattan, his name was inscribed on the tablets of the sea — he had entered what would be called the Hudson River.

Hudson was not the first to discover the mouth of the river; the Italian explorer Giovanni da Verrazano had been there in 1524 as had the Portuguese mariner, Estevan Gomez, in the same year. But these men did little more than bring back vague reports of the existence of a large harbor. Hudson sailed up the river as far north as present-day Albany and his detailed description of the great harbor and inland water route did much to encourage settlers to develop the area today known as the Hudson River Valley.

Most of Hudson's journal describing his third voyage has been lost, and it is from Juet's diary that we learn of the difficult days that followed. Four days after they had anchored in the entrance to the harbor, Coleman and four crew members were attacked by Indians. Coleman was killed by an arrow that pierced his throat. Juet does not explain the cause of the attack, he only tells us that the mysterious onslaught of arrows proved that the Indians were savages who could not be trusted.

In the few pages of Hudson's journal that have been preserved, he wrote about the Indians in a kindly way. Yet he ordered barricades placed over the portholes, made his men carry firearms, and stationed a permanent lookout. Furthermore, when the Indians came to trade, he captured two of them as hostages, hoping their presence would discourage further attacks; and he did nothing to discourage the crew from dressing the Indians in ridiculous outfits and parading them up and down the deck like clowns.

As the *Half Moon* sailed up the river, Hudson made careful charts of the area and took frequent soundings to determine the depth of the water. He tested the speed of the current and even noted the sandbars and whirlpools he encountered. By mid-September the Palisades, near present-day West Point, were sighted. "Nature was in one of her happier moods when she created these cliffs," Hudson wrote in his log, and then described the landscape in detail. He was anxious to send a party of men ashore, but, according to Juet, he was afraid. "It having been proved to our sorrow that the natives hereabouts are bloodthirsty, I dare not. . . ." Juet quoted Hudson's words. After the fifteenth, Hudson became even more cautious, because the two hostages escaped.

Three days later, however, his fears seemed to vanish. We know that he sailed to shore in an Indian canoe, in his own words, "with an old man who was the chief of a tribe of forty men and seventeen women; these I saw there in a house well-constructed of oak bark and circular in shape. . . . On our coming into the house . . . immediately some food was served in well-made red wooden bowls . . . ." In describing the meal, Hudson explained that the Indians "killed a fat dog. . . . Then they roasted it, and when it was cooked they cut pieces of meat from the carcass with shell knives and ate it with their fingers."

Hudson continued his journey up river as far as the site of Albany. "The land is the finest for cultivation that I ever in my

Indians of New York.

36

life set foot upon," he wrote, "and it abounds in trees of every description. But the water was becoming increasingly more shallow, and Hudson soon realized that this river, which became known by his name, was not the sea route to the East.

On September 23, the *Half Moon* began her homeward voyage, and within a week the little vessel reached the location of present-day Poughkeepsie. Unfortunately, the crew decided to stop to trade for furs. One Indian climbed onto the rudder of the ship, and as luck would have it, he ended up in the nasty Juet's cabin. When the first mate discovered that the Indian had stolen his pillow, two swords, and two shirts he became so furious that he shot the thief. The other Indians panicked at the sound of the gunfire and leaped overboard. Then, the crew, fearing that they too had been robbed, went after the Indians; one Indian was hacked to death in his attempt to escape. The following morning the *Half Moon* continued down river, but the episode was not closed. The Indians returned to take revenge. Before the ship was in range of their arrows, however, their band was sighted. Juet ordered the cannons fired. Five or six Indians were killed and a number drowned; the rest scattered. It was a sad ending to Hudson's stay in America, but it was only a small sample of what was to come when the white man returned to settle the Indian's land.

We know little of Hudson's return voyage. The last entry in Juet's diary was on October 4, when he notes that "we set our sayles . . . and steered away . . . into the mayne sea."

On November 7, 1609, the *Half Moon* reached England. During the trip there had apparently been some trouble on board, for the Dutch sailors were unwilling to return to Holland. Hudson, therefore, ordered the ship's anchor dropped in the harbor of Dartmouth. In so doing, his third and most important voyage came to an end.

THE TABLETS OF THE SEA

Upon his return to England, Hudson was more certain than ever that if he could undertake just one more voyage, he would find the passage to the East. Without delay, he sent an account of his trip to the directors of the East India Company and, in the same letter, he requested that they finance another voyage in the spring. Due to a storm at sea, however, the letter did not reach Holland until December. Early in January, the company sent word to Hudson to report to Amsterdam. But by the time the letter arrived, Hudson and the entire English crew had been forbidden to leave the country without special permission from King James I. "From the moment we encountered the king's men we were held under close arrest," wrote Juet. For according to King James, Hudson and his crew had betrayed their country by sailing under the Dutch flag.

Fortunately for Hudson, three influential English merchants took an interest in his travels: Sir Thomas Smith, Sir Dudley Digges, and John Wolstenholme. With the help of these men and the backing of the king's eldest son, Henry, prince of Wales, a new company was formed to finance Hudson's fourth voyage.

The winter of 1610 must have been most exciting for Hudson. The prince had spoken to his father and the king had agreed to remove the guards from Hudson's house. The merchants who backed Hudson gave him the freedom to chart his own course, and he had no restrictions placed on ordering supplies. He was given an excellent ship, the bark *Discovery*: it was a broad-beamed

*King James I of England
portrayed on a medal
commemorating the
peace with Spain in 1604.*

ship with an extremely sturdy hull that Hudson knew would protect the ship when they encountered drifting ice.

Unfortunately, as we have seen, Hudson was a poor judge of men and the twenty-three member crew he chose for his fourth voyage was even more troublesome than the one for the voyage before. The first man he hired was Robert Juet. Even after all the problems Juet had created, for some unknown reason, Captain Hudson decided upon him as his mate.

Another mysterious selection was Henry Greene. This handsome young rogue was even worse than Juet. He was a violent, quarrelsome, and treacherous man whose friends were the criminals of London. Hudson not only gave him a job, but made him his favorite, constantly giving him special treatment. The other crew members were a more honest lot, perhaps, but hardly could be called an outstanding group of seamen. As on the previous voyages, young John Hudson accompanied his father.

The preparations for the voyage went smoothly and in record time the *Discovery* was ready to set sail. In the early hours of the morning of April 17, 1610, Hudson bid England his final farewell.

From the outset, the voyage seemed ill fated. Before the *Discovery* had sailed into the mouth of the Thames, Hudson fired a man named Coleburne. Though one of the crew named Abacuk Prickett kept a careful account of the trip, he does not explain why Coleburne was sent ashore and Hudson's own incomplete account makes no mention of the incident.

By the last week of May, the *Discovery* reached the coast of Iceland. Severe storms and thick fog made it impossible to continue sailing and the entire crew spent the next fourteen days ashore. This was when the trouble began. Henry Greene had a terrible fight with the ship's doctor, Edward Wilson. Then, Wilson refused to return to the ship. It was only after much persuasion by the others that he finally agreed to go back on board.

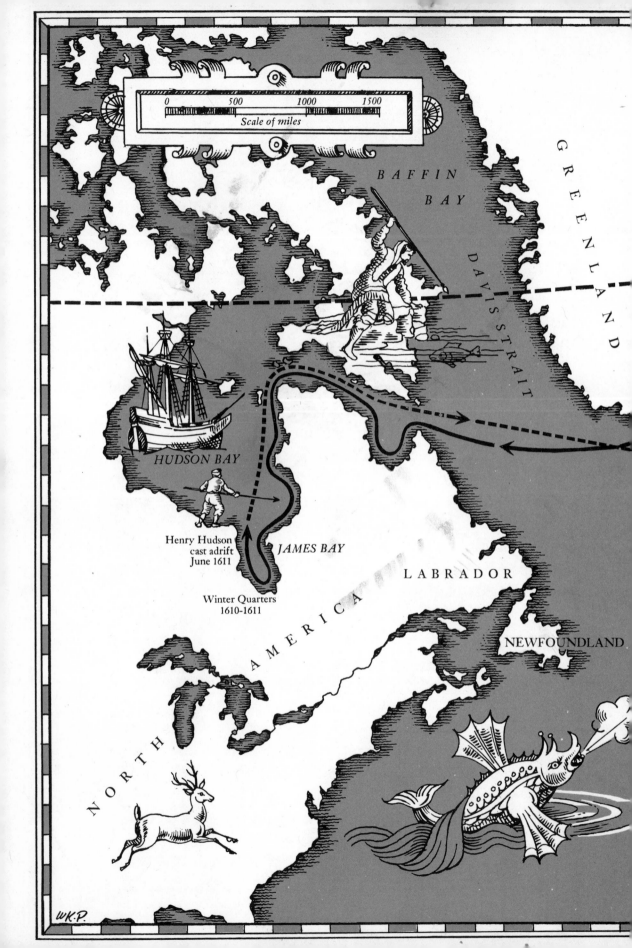

BAFFIN
BAY

GREENLAND

DAVIS STRAIT

HUDSON BAY

Henry Hudson
cast adrift
June 1611

JAMES BAY

Winter Quarters
1610-1611

LABRADOR

NEWFOUNDLAND

NORTH

AMERICA

Scale of miles

0   500   1000   1500

W.K.P.

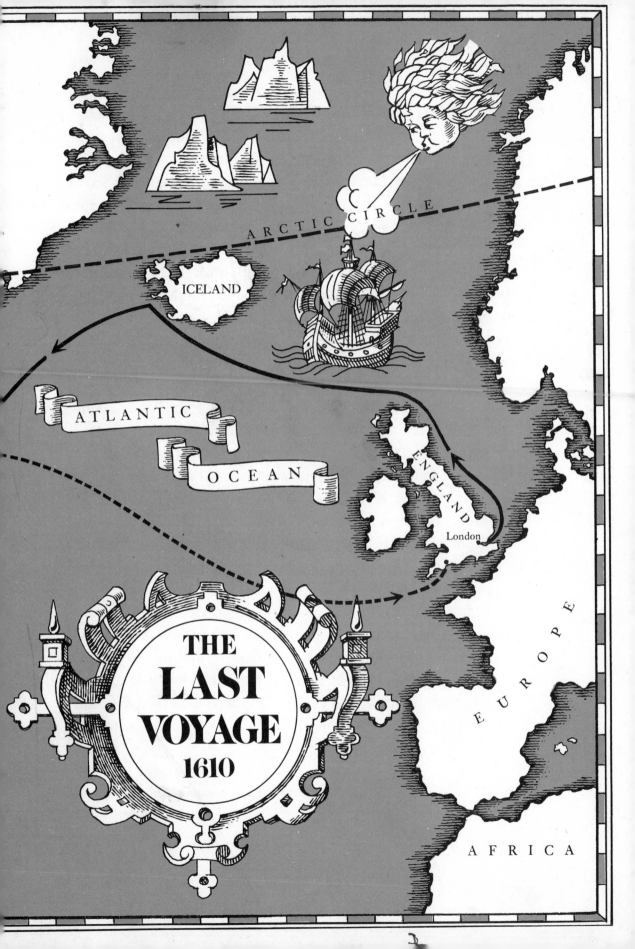

ARCTIC CIRCLE

ICELAND

ATLANTIC

OCEAN

ENGLAND

London

EUROPE

AFRICA

THE
LAST
VOYAGE
1610

Next, Juet, the arch intriguer, began to make trouble. He was jealous of Greene and angry that Hudson favored the young "spy" as he called him, and so he set out to turn the crew against their captain. Hudson did not discover the plot until after the ship was again underway. He threatened to return to Iceland and leave Juet behind; but the clever mate apologized and Hudson, having no other seaman to replace him, let the incident pass.

By the beginning of June they had passed Greenland and Frobisher Bay. Then, according to Prickett, on June 24, at exactly midnight, the swift currents of the Furious Overfall pulled the little bark through Romles Inlet into the 450-mile-long body of water that became known as Hudson Strait.

For years Hudson had dreamed of reaching the Furious Overfall. He was certain that the rushing currents they encountered were created by the strong tides of some great sea; he was convinced that the sea was the Pacific. Hudson was not the first to reach these waters, but he was the first to navigate through the hundred-mile-long strait that separates the northern cape of Labrador from the southern tip of Baffin Island.

It took Hudson over a month to manoeuvre around the enormous islands of ice that floated in the strait. But finally, on August 3, they reached Cape Digges — named by Hudson in honor of his sponsor — and anchored at the entrance to a narrow channel. Just imagine the excitement of the crew when the three men who went ashore came back with reports that from the top of a cliff they had seen an unending body of water. Hudson was certain they had reached the Pacific; until now, no map had in any way indicated the existence of this body of water, to be called Hudson Bay.

A man fishing in the area
north of Hudson Bay.

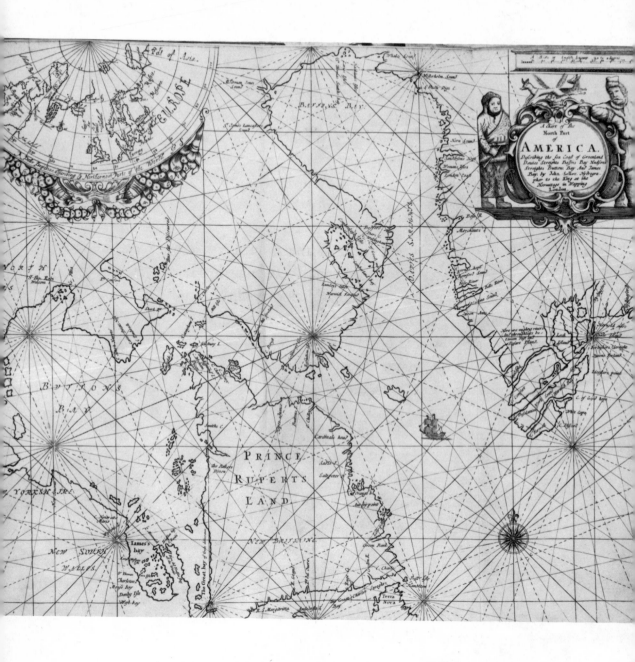

*A map of the north area of the
American continent drawn in 1671.
Button's Bay was later
renamed Hudson Bay.*

During the month of September, they sailed due south, charting the newly found coastline. The weather was becoming increasingly cold, the icefields more and more hazardous, and the dangers of approaching winter were a constant threat to the men. Hudson, however, was certain that he would reach the Orient by February; he could not be convinced to stop even long enough to catch fresh game.

By the beginning of November, the *Discovery* reached the southeast corner of James Bay, which is really an extension of Hudson Bay, and by the third of the month, the crew realized that they were iced in for the winter. Once again Henry Greene began to fight with Dr. Wilson; Hudson foolishly took Greene's side, opening the door for Juet to begin sowing seeds of mutiny. "We shall all be at the bottom of the sea . . . if he persists in his madness," he kept telling the crew.

The months ahead were gruesome. The men were starving and many were suffering from scurvy — their joints were swollen and they were crippled with pain. "We ate moss, then which I take the powder of a post [sawdust] to be much better," wrote Prickett. One day the ship's gunner, John William, wandered into the wilderness looking for game. His frozen body was found the next morning.

In the seventeenth century, it was customary to auction a dead seaman's clothes. Hudson allowed no bidding; instead he gave his favorite, Greene, the gunner's warm overcoat. A few days later, however, Greene disobeyed Hudson. In an outburst of temper, the angry captain took back the coat and gave it to Robert Bylot, his new mate — Juet had, by this time, been demoted to an ordinary seaman. The episode ended, but the discontent continued. "To speake of all our trouble in this time of winter (which was so cold as it lamed the most of our company, and myselfe doe yet feele it) would be too tedious," wrote Prickett.

A Journal of a voyage Intended (by Gods permission)
in the George of London, A B commander from the
Lezard in Lahtud: 50° 10′ North, Long: 9° 40 m To the
Island Barbadoes in Lat 13° 20′ North. Longd 317° 40 m
Their Differenc of Longd 52° course 49° 13′ S W Distance
3397 mmls Kept by C D chief Mate. Begun Jan: 716
1605

			Zenith Dist	D. M			E §
Merid Dist in Dgℯ mils	Longd by Accℓ in Degre mℓs		Declination . .		May Ampl 20 30	
02. 08 W.	09. 40				Truℯ Amp 28 40	
	06. 29		Lat by observacö		variaton a 10	

As the weeks wore on, the situation worsened. Hudson claimed that it was Bylot's fault that the food supply was so low. Bylot was demoted and at once joined forces with those who opposed Hudson. The captain chose the carpenter, John King, as his first mate.

With the coming of spring, the ice began to thaw, crack, and separate. In one day the men caught over 500 fish. At last there was food for everyone. Hudson, however, neglected to have the fish salted and by the following day the catch began to rot. Then, for some reason, practically no fish could be netted. Again the hungry men began to grumble at their captain.

In June, after being iced in for seven and a half months, the *Discovery* was able to set sail. On the seventeenth, Hudson ordered the crew to weigh anchor. The men wanted to return to England, but Hudson still dreamed of finding a northwest passage so he steered the *Discovery* westward. This was the beginning of the end.

The crew felt that they had endured the pangs of hunger long enough. Their skin was pale, their cheeks hollow, and they looked like skeletons as they limped about the deck. Hudson was confident that they would soon find food. And so, as soon as they were underway, he brought out the remaining bread and cheese. The sparse amount was frightening. Rumors spread quickly that Hudson was hoarding large quantities for himself. At the same time, Hudson accused some of the men of hiding bread and he had the entire crew searched. Only thirty small cakes were found. A few days later Philip Staffe, the ship's carpenter, was caught eating pickled beef. To protect himself, he said that Hudson had given him the food. The crew was furious, especially Greene,

Left, an early example of a ship's log, or sailing record, kept in the form of a journal.

Over, a map of the world drawn by Joannes Janisjonius in Amsterdam, 1632.

who had devoured his rations within the first two days, and now faced starvation.

Three days later, Greene — whom Hudson had so favored — and William Wilson — the boatswain, not the doctor — had a secret meeting with Prickett. Juet, of course, was in on their plot. "They told me that they and the rest of the associates, would shift the company, and turne the Master, and all the sicke men into the shallop, and let them shift for themselves," Prickett wrote in his diary. He then explained that he tried to change their minds, but it is doubtful that this was out of loyalty to Hudson. It seems more likely that he was afraid of what would happen to him when he returned to England. Prickett emphasized that he had no choice, he had to join the others, or else Greene said, "I must take my fortune in the shallop."

The following morning, June 23, 1611, the mutineers were ready. Greene seized Hudson and bound him with a long rope. A small boat was lowered and Hudson, his teen-age son, John, and seven sick sailors were forced aboard. The carpenter, John King, was included, "for the Master loved him and made him his Mate," Prickett wrote.

As the mutineers lowered the shallop into the water, Philip Staffe shouted that he would rather sink than mutiny. Refusing to stay on board, he joined Hudson. Once Staffe was in the shallop the mutineers cut the line and the small boat quickly disappeared from sight. But a little while later, the shallop came back into view. The crew panicked, Prickett explained, "they let fall the main-sayle, and out with their top-sayles, and flye as from an enemy."

Three and a half centuries have passed since the small boat drifted into the horizon. What happened to Henry Hudson and his young son John? What was the fate of Philip Staffe and John King? How long were seven sick men able to survive with neither food nor fresh water? There are no answers. Even if they did not die at sea, their ending must have been a tragic one; they could not have lived for any length of time in the wilderness of the north.

But the fate of the mutineers was not much better. As soon as the shallop was out of sight, the men searched the ship and, according to Prickett, they found a private stock of food in Hudson's room. Bylot was then elected head of the ship and with the men in good spirits, he sailed the *Discovery* northward. When they reached Cape Digges, the men managed to catch thirty birds. A feast was held. This was the last of the merrymaking. After devouring the birds, the men cooked the bones and feathers in candlegrease. For the next two months they lived on a diet of candles-in-vinegar.

Hudson had warned the mutineers that misfortune lay ahead. He was right. By the time the *Discovery* sailed through the straits, the thirteen men aboard were weak with hunger. Bylot had to use a whip to force his starving crew to work. Off the coast of Labrador an Eskimo camp was sighted. The men went ashore hoping to secure food. Instead of trying to trade fairly, they set out to take what they wanted by force. Greene was killed by an Eskimo spear. Prickett was badly wounded and the Eskimo fishermen cut out the bowels of two men and stabbed a third to death.

The days ahead were little better. Juet died "for mere want" before reaching Iceland, wrote Prickett. Then, "with eight men aboarde we did at last reach England." The leaders were all dead.

Upon their return, Bylot and Prickett convinced the king that they had discovered a northwest passage and became members of a new company called "The Discoverers of the North West." Bylot returned to Hudson Bay in 1617, but finally admitted that he could not find an outlet to the Pacific. The other six mutineers were imprisoned. Their trial was not held until 1618, at which time they were found "not guilty" and released.

As for Hudson's widow, Katherine, she was given a small pension and a job in the London offices of the English East India Company. But it was not until 1622, two years before her death, that she was honored as the wife of a great explorer. During the last months of her life she tried to raise funds to erect a memorial to her husband. She did not succeed.

But the world did not need a statue to remember the work of Captain Henry Hudson. His name became a symbol of courage and perseverance. Though he made no great discoveries, the importance of his explorations cannot be underestimated. He had proved that it was not possible to sail across the Pole from West to East; he was responsible for England's entry into the profitable whaling industry; as a result of his third voyage, he laid claim to the fertile Hudson Valley in the name of the Dutch; and for England, he claimed the vast territory of land surrounding Hudson Bay.

More than three hundred and sixty years have passed since the tragic death of Henry Hudson, but his greatest wish has not been forgotten. The Hudson River, Hudson Strait, and Hudson Bay are the realization of this daring navigator's dream. They remind us of the man who in 1607 had written: "I pray with all my heart . . . that my name be carved on the tablets of the sea."

A NOTE ON SOURCES

The Original Documents, Henry Hudson (published by Burt Franklin) are the basic reference source for the explorer's life. A helpful biography is *Henry Hudson* by Llewelyn Powys.

THE AUTHOR

Joan Joseph is a graduate of McGill University and has studied at the University of Southern California, the Universite d'Aix-Marseille, and the University of Paris. She holds a foundation grant for historical research on thirteenth-century England, which she is presently pursuing in London. Joan Joseph is the author of several books for young people.

INDEX